The Official
Heart of Midlothian
Football Club
Annual 2010

Written By Paul Kiddie

A Grange Publication

© 2009. Published by Grange Communications Ltd., Edinburgh, under licence from Heart of Midlothian Football Club plc. Printed in the EU.

Photographs © SNS Group

ISBN 978-1-906211-79-0

£6.99

CONTENTS
2010

CLUB STATS

HEART OF MIDLOTHIAN FC THE HEART AND SOUL OF EDINBURGH

FORMED 1874

CHAMPIONS 1895, 1897, 1958, 1960

SCOTTISH CUP 1891, 1896, 1901, 1906, 1956, 1998, 2006

LEAGUE CUP 1954-55, 1958-59, 1959-60, 1962-63

1ST DIVISION CHAMPIONS 1980

RECORD VICTORY 21-0 V. ANCHOR EFA CUP: 30.10.1880

MOST CAPS STEVEN PRESSLEY, 32 FOR SCOTLAND

MOST LEAGUE APPEARANCES GARY MACKAY - 515 (1980-97)

MOST LEAGUE GOALS JOHN ROBERTSON - 214 (1983-98)

MOST LEAGUE GOALS IN A SEASON BARNEY BATTLES - 44 (1930-31)

OFFICIAL WEBSITE WWW.HEARTSFC.CO.UK

OFFICIAL MOBILE SITE HEARTSFC.WAP.COM

OFFICIAL STORE WWW.HEARTSDIRECT.CO.UK

OFFICIAL ONLINE TV CHANNEL WWW.HEARTS.TV

ROLL OF HONOUR

SCOTTISH CHAMPIONS: 1894-95; 1896-97; 1957-58; 1959-60

SCOTTISH LEAGUE RUNNERS-UP: 1893-94; 1898-99; 1903-04; 1905-06; 1914-15; 1937-38; 1953-57; 1958-59; 1964-65

SCOTTISH PREMIER DIVISION RUNNERS-UP: 1985-86; 1987-88; 1991-92

SCOTTISH PREMIER LEAGUE RUNNERS-UP: 2005-06

SCOTTISH FIRST DIVISION CHAMPIONS: 1979-80

SCOTTISH FA CUP WINNERS: 1890-91; 1895-96; 1900-01; 1905-06; 1955-56; 1997-98; 2005-06

SCOTTISH FA CUP FINALISTS: 1902-03; 1906-07; 1967-68; 1975-76; 1985-86; 1995-96

SCOTTISH LEAGUE WINNERS: 1954-55; 1958-59; 1959-60; 1962-63

SCOTTISH LEAGUE CUP FINALISTS: 1961-62; 1996-97

VICTORY CUP FINALISTS: 1918-19

SCOTTISH LEAGUE EAST & NORTH DIVISION RUNNERS-UP: 1939-40

SCOTTISH SOUTHERN LEAGUE CUP FINALISTS: 1940-41

TEXACO CUP FINALISTS: 1970-71

PASSPORT
TO EUROPE

Season 2008
REVIEW

All eyes were on Tynecastle as Csaba Laszlo took his place in the home dugout for the first game of the season. Expectations were high, and the punters who flocked to Gorgie weren't disappointed as the Jambos edged a five-goal thriller.

Michael Stewart got proceedings off to a superb start with a fine solo effort only for the Steelmen to be back on level terms within 10 minutes through David Clarkson.

As the interval approached Audrius Ksanavicius pounced to restore the hosts' advantage. With the clock ticking down, his strike looked like being enough to secure victory only for Well to snatch an equaliser with nine minutes remaining. The pulsating encounter wasn't finished, though, and straight from the kick-off Hearts raced upfield and Saulius Mikoliunas blasted home a spectacular winner. What a start to the season!

30.8.08
Hamilton 1, Hearts 2

Hearts continued their impressive opening to the Clydesdale Bank Premier League campaign with victory over newly promoted Accies at New Douglas Park.

Marius Zaliukas headed the visitors in front early in the opening period, with Andrew Driver doubling the advantage after the break. Although Derek Lyle handed his side a late lifeline, the Maroons saw out the remaining minutes to record a deserved win.

Given the form of Billy Reid's side in the first half of the season, it was a hugely valuable three points.

19.10.08
Hibs 1, Hearts 1

The clash at Easter Road was noteworthy because of the memorable return to first-team action of Bruno Aguiar after a year-and-a-half out with injury.

Trailing to an early Steven Fletcher goal, Hearts levelled the match in sensational style in the first half, with the Portuguese midfielder stepping forward to smash an unstoppable free kick past the helpless Ma-Kalambay. Bruno was back!

8.11.08
St Mirren 0, Hearts 1

Hearts' last visit to Love Street before the bulldozers moved in was to prove a fruitful one, Eggert Jonsson the match winner with his header 12 minutes from time.

The hard-fought victory was all the more creditable given the fact the visitors were forced to play the entire second half with 10 men after Michael Stewart was sent off following an incident with Hugh Murray as the interval approached.

Another big positive from the game was the return of defensive stalwart Robbie Neilson after a lengthy spell on the sidelines.

The victory was Hearts' first since September 20 but triggered an impressive run of five straight wins in the league to send out a message to their SPL rivals.

...an impressive run of five straight wins!!

29.11.08
Hearts 2, Rangers 1

The Glasgow side arrived in Gorgie knowing they were in for a tough 90 minutes, with Hearts having won their previous four matches.

By the time Marius Zaliukas and Laryea Kingston had fired a quick-fire double in the first half, the foundations for a fifth successive victory had been well-established.

An own goal from Christos Karipidis moments later breathed life into the visitors, but the home side did well to maintain their advantage despite Lee Wallace seeing red 15 minutes from time.

Season REVIEW 2008/09

13.12.08
Celtic 1, Hearts 1

The Jambos proved that the fantastic victory over Rangers was no fluke with another impressive result against the other half of the Old Firm at Parkhead.

A cracking drive from Andrew Driver midway through the first half gave Hearts the lead, much to the delight of the travelling support. The flying winger was only denied a second shortly after by a superb save from Artur Boruc.

The home side eventually managed to peg back their in-form visitors, when Stephen McManus netted from close range.

17.1.09
Kilmarnock 0, Hearts 2

Hearts made the trip to Rugby Park and recorded their first league victory of the season by more than two goals.

On the hour mark, Portuguese midfielder Bruno Aguiar lit up what had been a dull encounter in dreadful conditions with a rasping drive, the effort setting Hearts on the way to another valuable win on the road.

Christos Karipidis completed the scoring with a close-range effort to send the fans back home from Ayrshire in buoyant mood.

24.1.09
Hearts 3, Inverness CT 2

It may have taken a long time coming but David Obua netted his first goal for Hearts since signing from South African side Kaizer Chiefs in the summer against the Highlanders – and promptly followed up with his second!

The visitors made their hosts battle all the way, however, and after equalising for a second time with just two minutes remaining they appeared to have done enough to return north with a point.

Hearts had other ideas, though, and Laryea Kingston popped up with the perfect reply straight from the kick-off when he converted Andrew Driver's cutback.

The game was also to prove captain Christophe Berra's last in maroon, the defender signing for Wolves before the transfer window closed.

14.2.09
Hearts 2, Aberdeen 1

The meeting on St Valentine's Day was eagerly anticipated by both sets of fans, although things didn't start too well for the home side with the Dons taking the lead in the first half through Darren Mackie.

Hearts, though, levelled things on the stroke of half-time when Christian Nade finished off a superb move.

The winner the Gorgie faithful craved arrived courtesy of Andrew Driver in the second half, the three points taking the Jambos back into third place.

Season REVIEW 2008/09

28.2.09
Dundee United 0, Hearts 1

Michael Stewart was the hero for the Tynecastle side at one end of the pitch – and Janos Balogh was a saviour at the other end.

The midfielder pounced in the second half to net the only goal of the game, the victory sending the Jambos five points clear in third place.

Gorgie No. 1 Balogh ensured another fruitful away day for the Edinburgh club when he saved a late penalty from Francisco Sandaza.

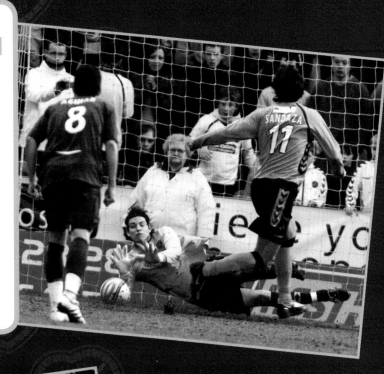

4.3.09
Hearts 2, Motherwell 1

The Edinburgh club staged another stunning finale under the Tynecastle floodlights, Ruben Palazuelos' deflected shot grabbing victory in stoppage time.

After a goal-less first half, Hearts took the lead with a headed effort from Andrew Driver.

Stephen Hughes smashed a great leveller for the Steelmen with just 15 minutes remaining, and, just when it seemed Mark McGhee's side would escape back to Lanarkshire with a share of the spoils, Palazuelos was on hand with his dramatic contribution to cement his side's third place position in the Clydesdale Bank Premier League.

21.3.09
Rangers 2, Hearts 2

There aren't many teams who can give Rangers a two-goal half-time advantage at Ibrox and take anything from the game.

Hearts, though, could count themselves unfortunate not to actually win the match after a Calum Elliot-inspired fightback after the break.

Goals from Christos Karipidis and Ruben Palazuelos stunned the home support and only the fingertips of Allan McGregor prevented substitute Elliot from securing a famous victory in the closing seconds of the pulsating encounter.

T♥GETHER

11.4.09
Hearts 1, Celtic 1

No sooner had the game kicked off than the Jambos were trailing, the Parkhead side having opened the scoring through Jan Vennegoor of Hesselink.

It was a nightmare start for the hosts but they came storming back and equalised through another of Bruno Aguiar's trademark free kicks, the midfielder leaving Artur Boruc sprawling with a magnificent curling effort.

Both teams could have won it after the break but had to settle for a point apiece, the Jambos demonstrating once again they could mix it with the best.

16.5.09
Hearts 3, Dundee United 0

Billed as the shoot-out for third place in the Clydesdale Bank Premier League, Hearts picked the perfect match in which to produce their best performance of the season.

Craig Levein's Tangerines were simply swept aside by a rampant home team, the Jambos cruising to victory in impressive fashion.

Two up after just 25 minutes through goals from Lee Wallace and Bruno Aguiar, there was little doubt as to the destiny of the three points, and the Maroons completed a convincing victory when Eggert Jonsson converted from the penalty spot 12 minutes from time.

24.5.09
Celtic 0, Hearts 0

The Tynecastle side completed a highly successful campaign with another encouraging performance at a packed Celtic Park on the final day of the season.

The stalemate was Hearts' third successive draw against the Glasgow giants and underlined the new-found resolve being enjoyed under Csaba Laszlo.

David Templeton made his first start for the club, while fellow youngsters Arvydas Novikovas and Jonathan Stewart made their top-team debuts from the bench in the second half.

Season
REVIEW 2008/09

Jose Goncalves

WORD SEARCH

Can you find the 10 current Hearts players?

```
U Z H T O P E G X K N X
K C Y P H F A G L E N F
E C V A J O N S S O N V
O J D L D B M Y G O M I
B Z R A M M L S D Q G K
U E L Z E S O A O W G I
A X V U H M T L C N S B
K T E E B I J E E K J Q
B R R L K D Y E W H R Y
K M Y O O B Z P X A K S
Y T I S S W T L S I R O
S S A G B A L O G H S T
```

BALOGH	STEWART	JONSSON	GLEN	MOLE
OBUA	DRIVER	THOMSON	BLACK	PALAZUELOS

Answers on page 61.

GARY'S GOAL

Striker Gary Glen has insisted he doesn't want to be remembered by Hearts fans for THAT goal against Hibs.

The young front man carved himself a niche in Gorgie folklore with his sublime strike at Easter Road which sent the Hibees tumbling out of the Homecoming Scottish Cup last season.

His superb finish in front of the visiting support completed a 2-0 triumph for the Jambos and helped re-affirm the teenager as something of a fans' favourite at Tynecastle.

The 19-year-old certainly enjoyed the moment and the adulation which followed, but he is the first to admit that, while it is a moment he will remember fondly for a long time, he hopes to have people talking about more scoring exploits in the future.

"It is great to score against Hibs and the fact it came in the Scottish Cup made it even more pleasing," he said.

"The supporters certainly thought it was an extra special goal, and I have to say I have never experienced anything like that before. In some ways, though, it was just another one for the tally, and my aim is to keep scoring goals for the club when I get the chance."

"...the fact it came in the Scottish Cup made it even more pleasing..."

Some of the Gorgie faithful swept away by the euphoria of Glen's killer contribution at Easter Road began hailing the youngster as the 'new John Robertson'. But that is something which doesn't rest easily on the starlet's shoulders.

Well versed in the Tynecastle legend's heroics in front of goal, the young striker wants to be known simply as himself.

"I heard what all the fans were saying after that goal against Hibs last season," he said. "But I want to be known because of what I have done, not compared to a legend.

"Hopefully I will get the chance to prove myself to the manager. I am willing to work hard and wait for my opportunity and show the fans that it's not all about scoring in big games."

Glen burst onto the first-team scene in 2008 when he scored his first senior goal in a league victory over St Mirren at Tynecastle, and he went on to scoop the Clydesdale Bank Premier League Graduate Award.

With the arrival of a new manager in the form of Csaba Laszlo last summer, though, it was back to the drawing board in terms of impressing the gaffer, as the striker readily recognises.

"When the new boss came in I had to show what I could do," he said. "It is always hard when a new manager comes into a club, and he preferred one up top which is a role Christian Nade filled. Calum Elliot then came back from his loan at Livingston and did well, so I had to wait for my chance."

Glen missed the final couple of games of last season as Hearts secured third place in the table after undergoing surgery to his nose in May, former Tynecastle defender Andy Webster having caught him with his elbow during a reserve meeting with Rangers.

"There was nothing broken, but the cartilage was damaged and I was struggling to breathe so it was decided that an operation was required. It wasn't the best start to the summer!" he said.

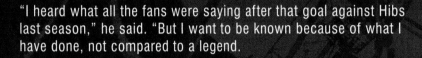

"... the young striker wants to be known simply as himself."

"...my aim is to keep scoring goals for the club..."

MAZE TO TYNECASTLE

Answers on page 61.

Dawid Kucharski

EURO VISIONS

PARTY TIME: Celebrations begin after Hearts see off the challenge of Braga in Portugal in the UEFA Cup 1st round, 2nd leg in 2004.

DOWN BUT NOT OUT: Phil Stamp takes a tumble during the 2003-04 UEFA Cup 1st round, 2nd leg clash against NK Zeljeznicar in Sarajevo.

LEAP OF FAITH: Craig Gordon keeps Siroki Brijeg at bay during the Champions League 2nd qualifying round, 2nd leg clash in the Pecara Stadium.

LEAD ROLE: Captain Colin Cameron in action against Stuttgart in a pulsating UEFA Cup tie at Tynecastle in September 2000.

MARK OF CLASS: Match-winner Mark de Vries gets to grips with Bordeaux in the 2nd round, 1st leg clash in France in November 2003.

BASEL BRUSHED AWAY: Hearts' heroes walk off after shocking Basel in the UEFA Cup group stages in November 2004.

GREAT GOAL: Iain Ferguson leaves Bayern Munich stunned with his fabulous free kick winner in the first leg of the UEFA Cup quarter-final at Tynecastle in February 1989.

REAL DEAL: Stefano Salvatori does battle with Real Mallorca during the 1st round, 1st leg Cup-Winners' Cup clash at Tynecastle in September 1998.

ANNUAL QUIZ

1 Against which team did Hearts open their Clydesdale Bank Premier League campaign last season?

2 Who scored Hearts' first league goal of last season?

3 What was significant about the 2-1 victory over Rangers at Tynecastle in November?

4 How many victories did Hearts record in the league last season?

5 Can you name the player who made his first-team debut against Celtic at Parkhead on the last day of the season?

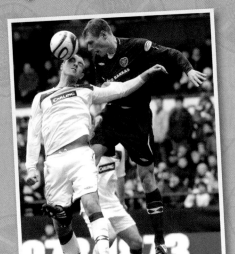

6 Which English team paid big money for Christophe Berra in January?

7 How many goals did Hearts score against Dundee United last season?

8 Andrew Driver scored his first goal of last season against whom?

9 At what ground did David Templeton make his first-team debut in May?

10 How many times did Jamie MacDonald play for Hearts against Rangers last season?

Answers on page 61.

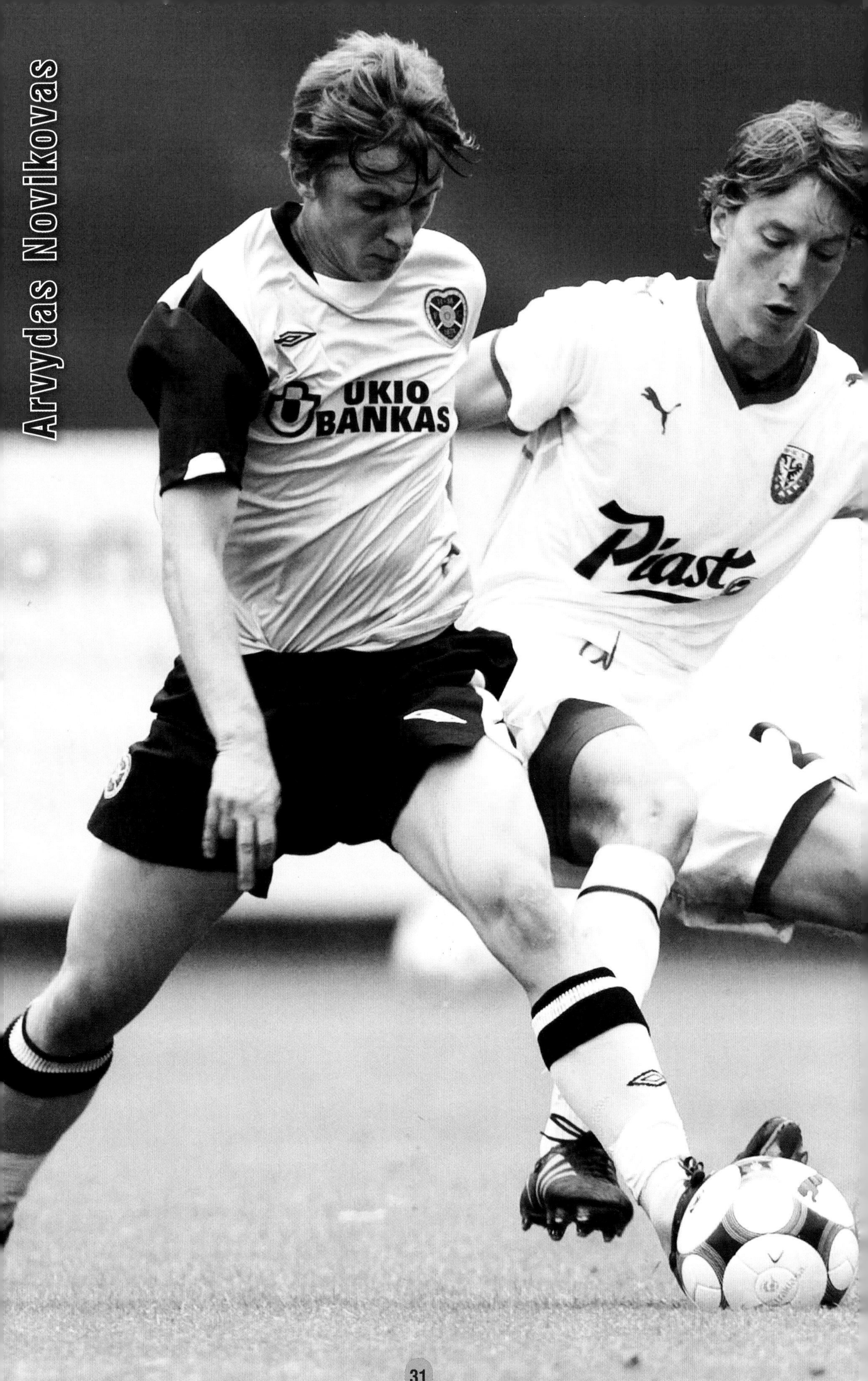

Arvydas Novikovas

NO REGRETS

The chance to join Benfica must have been tempting but youngster Arvydas Novikovas is adamant he made the right decision in pledging his future to Hearts.

The teenager had been on trial with the top Portuguese club from FK Vilnius and impressed sufficiently to be offered the chance of a deal in the summer of 2008.

However, when the Tynecastle club made its interest known, Novikovas knew his career path would take him to Edinburgh instead of the bright lights of Lisbon.

Many outside of Gorgie might have raised an eyebrow at the decision but the highly-rated Lithuanian U21 international is in no doubt it was the correct thing to do.

"Benfica wanted me to sign a contract with them, but I decided on Hearts, and I am happy that I made the right decision," he said.

"I knew it was the right decision to make for the sake of forwarding my career."

The Gorgie starlet impressed last season with the U19s and reserves and was given his chance with the first team on the final day of the Clydesdale Bank Premier League campaign when Hearts faced Celtic in front of a packed Parkhead.

His big moment came minutes into the second half when the signal came for him to get stripped for action from the substitutes' bench.

Looking back on the occasion at the end of May, Novikovas insists his involvement in such a high-profile fixture justified his decision to sign a three-year deal with Hearts.

"The game against Celtic was a great experience for me," he said. "To play in front of such a big crowd was a very special occasion, and I think it proves that I made the right decision to come to Hearts."

His stomach may have been churning as he looked on from the sidelines, but, having savoured the first-team experience, he is keen to see more this season.

"To play in front of such a big crowd was a very special occasion, and I think it proves that I made the right decision to come to Hearts."

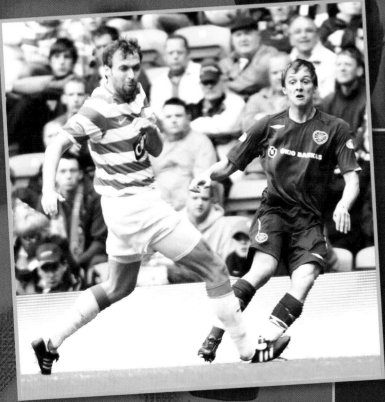

"The boss told me at half-time that I would be coming on after about five minutes or so, and I was very nervous waiting there for my opportunity," he said.

"To be honest the first few minutes were a bit scary, but after I got a few touches of the ball and got into the game it was fine. I was able to shut out the supporters and concentrate on what I was supposed to be doing on the pitch.

"I was a little bit surprised to play so much of the match, but I was delighted the boss showed faith in me. Obviously I would like to play more games for the first team, but first I must do consistently well for the Reserves, keep working hard and take things from there."

Q&A with RUBEN PALAZUELOS

Are you happy you made the decision to come to Hearts?
Coming to Scotland was a good opportunity for me. I had played with Racing Santander in the second division in Spain and then in Greece with Aris Salonika. I think it was a good decision as I am very happy here, the football is good and I'm enjoying it.

What's the biggest difference you have noticed about football in this country?
In Spain the football is more technical, and when you're in midfield it can be easier as you don't have pressure on the ball all the time. It is a physical game in Scotland, but, while it was difficult for me to begin with, I'm in my second year here now and think I have adapted well.

Has the move benefited you as a player?
I am a better footballer having moved to Hearts, for sure. I have learned to do a lot more with my game and that is good for me.

How frustrating were last season's injuries for you?
I got injured at the start of the year and then a knee injury caused me problems towards the end of last season. I had never really been injured before but this comes with a physical sport.

What was your reaction when you saw your picture fronting the season ticket campaign?
When I saw it above the ticket centre at Tynecastle, I was very happy! My brothers came over for a visit from Spain, and, once they knew about it, they wanted some photographs taken.

You are one of the more experienced players in the team this season. Do you enjoy that responsibility?
I'm 26 and have a responsibility to help the younger players at the club. I have an older brother and a younger one. I always speak to the younger one and give him advice. It is the same in football. When you have the experience, it is important to use it to help others as much as possible.

SPOT the DIFFERENCE

Can you spot the 6 differences?

Answers on page 61.

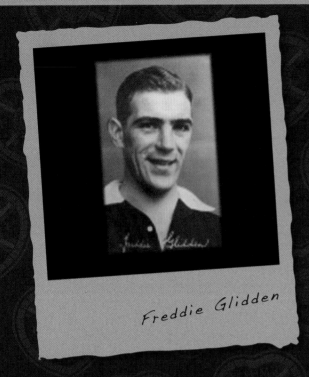

Freddie Glidden

FREDDIE GLIDDEN

Standing nearly six feet, Freddie was a powerful and intelligent centre-half and a star performer throughout the 1950s. He was born at Newmains in July 1928 but brought up in Stoneyburn, where he was spotted by Hearts playing juvenile football for Murrayfield Rovers. Freddie was signed provisionally in July 1945, and, after spells with West Calder Home Guard XI. and Whitburn Juniors, he was farmed out to Newtongrange Star. He had real presence at right-half or centre-half and earned two international caps for Scotland in the Junior Grade. He was called up to Tynecastle in 1948 and made his first-team breakthrough in 1951, eventually recording 270 appearances and scoring 3 goals (229 being competitive matches). The big defender was a part-time player during much of his career, combining football with his job in the West Lothian Water Board, but, he never lacked stamina or commitment. Freddie helped Hearts to win the League Cup in both October 1954 and October 1958 and he was also a member of the squad that won the League Championship in 1957-58. His greatest moment, however, came in 1956 when he captained the team to victory over Celtic in the Scottish Cup Final. Freddie played in Hearts' first European Cup matches and was four times a reserve for Scotland prior to joining Dumbarton in March 1959. He retired in 1962 and was later a sub postmaster for over 20 years.

STEVE FULTON

Steve was an outstanding playmaker and a hero of that memorable victory over Rangers in the Scottish Cup Final of 1998. The 5'11" midfielder was born at Greenock in August 1970 and his creative skills were first demonstrated with Celtic after he stepped up from Celtic Boys Club in May 1987. Steve earned seven U21 international honours and a Scottish Cup winner's medal before moving to Bolton Wanderers in July 1993 for a fee of £350,000. He then had a spell on loan to Peterborough United before a £100,000 move to Falkirk in August 1994. The influential midfielder helped the Bairns to stay in the Premier Division, before coming to Tynecastle in October 1995 in an exchange deal involving David Hagen. Steve then demonstrated his full range of skills and was rewarded with B international honours as he became a vital element in the Hearts team. Steve's consistently fine form was rewarded with the captaincy of the team in the 1998 Scottish Cup Final and he led by example in that famous encounter with Rangers. It was his surging run that brought the penalty that set Hearts on the road to victory. He also played for Hearts in the Scottish Cup Final in May 1996 and the League Cup Final in November 1996. In addition, Steve gained considerable experience in Europe and helped the club to third place in the Premier Division in seasons 1997-98 and 1999-2000. During the following campaign, he struggled with injuries and eventually moved to Kilmarnock in the summer of 2002 after scoring 22 goals in 268 games for Hearts (19/239 competitive). Steve later played for Partick Thistle before taking up coaching.

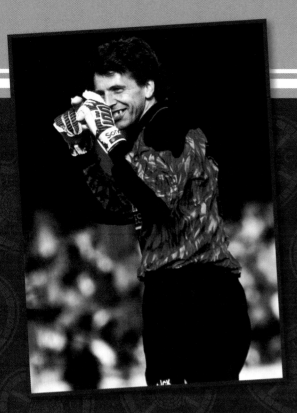

HENRY SMITH

Henry was an international-class goalkeeper who had safe hands, agility and great consistency. Only John Robertson and Gary Mackay can match his astonishing total of 701 games for Hearts. However, Henry's 214 shut-outs in 598 competitive games is a club record that could stand for all time. The 6'2" keeper was born in the Lanarkshire village of Rigside in March 1956, but he was raised in Hemsworth, Yorkshire, where he became a miner after leaving school. Henry also played football for Frickley Athletic and then Winterton Rangers, where a £10,000 fee took him to Leeds United. Henry found it difficult to make the breakthrough and was delighted when Tony Ford signed him for Hearts in July 1981 for a fee of £2,000. He immediately established his place in the team and was outstanding as Hearts won promotion from the First Division in 1982-83. Over the next decade, Henry's performances assisted Hearts to win a regular place in Europe. The popular keeper also helped the club to runners-up position in the League on three occasions (1985-86, 1987-88 and 1991-92) and to the 1986 Scottish Cup Final. He was a fixture at Tynecastle for nearly 15 years, and, at his peak, Henry was rewarded with three caps for Scotland, making his first appearance in February 1988 against Saudi Arabia. He also played for the U21 side as an over-age player. He richly deserved his testimonial in August 1993 against Everton. Henry went to Ayr United in January 1996 and he subsequently played for Glenafton Athletic Juniors, Gretna, Clydebank and Berwick Rangers where he was player-coach. Henry was later the manager of Whitehill Welfare and even played for Linlithgow Rose at the age of 49. He was one of the finest goalkeepers ever to appear for Hearts, and it would be impossible to calculate how many times Henry turned a game in our favour.

ALEX MACDONALD

Alex MacDonald is fondly remembered as the man who re-established Hearts' position as one of the leading clubs in Scotland, and his finest team almost secured the League and Cup Double in 1985-86. He was born in Glasgow in March 1948, although Alex commenced his senior career with St Johnstone, moving from Glasgow United to Perth in January 1966. Saints had a challenging team at that time and his midfield craft and regular goal-scoring earned a £50,000 transfer to Rangers in November 1968. The dynamic ball-winner went on to gain every domestic honour during his time at Ibrox and he was also a member of the famous Rangers side which won the European Cup-Winners' Cup in 1972. Alex played once for Scotland and he eventually signed for Hearts in August 1980 for £30,000. Alex became Hearts captain and the most influential player at the club, but it was too late to prevent relegation at the end of season 1980-81. After the departure of manager Tony Ford, the tough Glaswegian became player-coach in December 1981 and was then appointed player-manager in February 1982. The dynamic midfielder retired from playing in 1985 after scoring 21 goals in 181 games for Hearts (18 in 155 competitive matches). He restored the spirit of the club and led Hearts to promotion in 1982-83; back into European football the following season and almost to that sensational Double in 1985-86 when he was Scotland's Manager of the Year. From late 1986 to 1988, Alex shared the managerial role with his former assistant, Sandy Jardine, and Hearts were second in the League in 1987-88. Under his charge, big match action certainly returned to Tynecastle, and in 1989 Hearts defeated Bayern Munich in the quarter-final, first leg of the UEFA Cup. Alex left Hearts in September 1990 and had a successful spell in charge of Airdrieonians, taking them to two Scottish Cup Finals. In May 1984, Hearts and Rangers played a testimonial match in honour of Alex MacDonald's contribution to both clubs.

DECISION TIME

If Eggert Jonsson had not decided to pursue a career in football, there's every chance the Icelander would have been a success on the ski slopes.

Brought up in the small town of Eskifjordur on the east coast of the country, the keen sportsman used the winter months to hone his skills on the piste, while the summer time saw him charge around the football pitches.

As much as he enjoyed the thrills and spills of downhill skiing and competing for the national team, he couldn't resist the appeal of becoming a professional footballer.

When it eventually came to making a decision about his preferred career path, Jonsson admitted there wasn't any real soul searching to be done.

"I started downhill skiing when I was about five or six years old," he said. "In Iceland there can be heavy snow during the winter months so you can only do football training indoors.

"Up to around the age of 15, I used to ski in the winter most days and play football in the summer.

"But it got to the stage when I had to choose between skiing and football and in the end I went for the football.

"I'm not sure how realistic the downhill skiing would have been, even though I was quite good and made it into the Iceland national team, as I don't think our country's record was the best at that stage.

"The profile of either sport isn't the greatest, to be fair. It was hard at the time when I quit. The first time I did it, I came back to it for a year, but, while I enjoyed it, I realised football was the one for me and skiing more of a hobby."

"I think I was always going to choose
football ... I think I made the right choice!"

> *"I was always quite confident that football was the sport for me ..."*

Already a full internationalist and now established as a key member of the Hearts first team squad, the Tynecastle star clearly made the right decision.

"I had the potential to go and do something with my skiing, but, in the end, I think I was always going to choose football, and the skiing tailed off eventually. I think I made the right choice!" he said.

"My family still ski a lot and my younger sister trains quite hard, but it's not my interest any more.

"I was always quite confident that football was the sport for me, and I have been pleased with my development at Hearts. I have been here for four years now, started in the U19s and got to the Youth Cup Final in my first year, although we lost that one.

"The year after that, I was getting into the first team squad and made a few appearances so it was good to keep progressing. I got my first league start in the second game of the 2007-08 season in Aberdeen, kept working hard and eventually got a run in the team. It was the same last season although a little different as I was playing in a few different positions."

The Jambo ace, who turned 21 in August, proved his versatility last season as Hearts stormed to third place in the Clydesdale Bank Premier League, banishing memories of the previous season's disappointment in some style.

Jonsson admitted to being somewhat surprised at his own flexibility on the park.

"Playing in so many different positions will help me develop, so it has all been positive," he added.

"Looking back I can see my progress but I have to make sure that keeps happening as I am still young with a lot still to learn.

"I knew I had the ability to do something in the game, but I didn't realise I could play in so many different positions, and sometimes it's only when you are put in that situation that you realise what's possible."

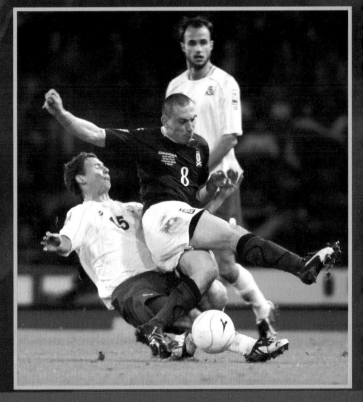

"Playing in so many different positions will help me develop, so it has all been positive."

WORD SEARCH

Can you find the 10 words associated with football?

E	N	C	H	W	C	G	P	H	I	K	F
O	I	D	S	V	O	F	F	S	I	D	E
A	T	T	B	D	Q	J	T	S	L	E	C
Z	E	H	D	J	W	N	E	R	D	R	R
A	C	J	X	T	M	A	A	E	A	A	R
J	B	O	R	B	F	A	H	F	B	M	C
D	B	J	Q	O	P	P	T	S	O	W	S
K	X	B	G	W	S	G	S	C	L	W	T
N	E	E	P	O	T	O	O	U	H	M	M
D	W	Q	M	F	R	K	O	A	G	U	Y
T	F	T	S	C	M	F	B	G	L	S	Q
I	A	C	B	R	P	E	N	A	L	T	Y

OFFSIDE   GOAL   PENALTY   FANS   FOUL

CROSSBAR   TEAMS   MATCH   BOX   ATMOSPHERE

Answers on page 61.

Ismael Bouzid

ONES TO WATCH

Arvydas
NOVIKOVAS

Born: 18.12.90

One of Lithuania's outstanding young talents, the teenager was attracting interest from some of Europe's top clubs before Hearts lured him to Tynecastle at the start of last season.

A frequent goal-scorer for both the U19s and Reserves, he made his first-team debut against Celtic at Parkhead on the final day of last season when he came off the bench early in the second half.

He can play on the left or right-hand side of midfield or off the strikers.

"One of Lithuania's outstanding young talents..."

Paul
MULROONEY

Born: 27.1.90

The midfielder has been with the club since the age of 12 and is another player highly rated by the coaches at the Football Academy.

Hailing from Bishopbriggs, he has impressed everybody with his attitude both on the training ground and on the pitch.

Another who is expected to make the step up to senior level in time, Paul has demonstrated great athleticism while performing well for Darren Murray's U19s last season.

"...highly rated by the coaches at the Football Academy."

ONES TO WATCH:

Jamie
WALKER

Born: 25.6.93

Academy Director John Murray has seen many young Hearts players progress to become stars in the game, and he believes the club has unearthed another gem in the shape of the 16-year-old striker.

Part of the youth system since he was nine years of age, the Wester Hailes lad has caught the eye with his all-round ability, and he has shown himself to be a finisher of some class with his strikes last season.

Despite his tender years, he will be hoping to make an impact with the U19s this season.

"...has shown himself to be a finisher of some class with his strikes last season."

Craig
THOMSON

Born: 17.4.91

Scooped the U19 Player of the Year award last season after consistently impressing at both that level and with the Reserves.

A genuine talent at right-back, he can also make a contribution further up the park as well. His deliveries from the wide areas are superb, while his ability from dead ball situations represents a great weapon.

He has impressed his coaches with his will to win. Was in the squad for the last game of the season against Celtic but failed to make the bench. He is expected to push for first-team recognition this season.

"He has impressed his coaches with his will to win."

At home with JANOS BALOGH

Where is your home town?
I come from Debrecen, which is around 100 miles or so to the east of the capital Budapest. It is the second largest city in Hungary.

How long did you live there?
I was there until 25 so pretty much my entire life.

How often do you get home?
The nature of football is that you don't get the chance to go home that often during the season. But this summer I went back to see all my friends and family.

Tell us some of the places a tourist should visit there?
The Second World War took its toll on the city. It suffered a lot of damage, but thankfully it has recovered well. It is a colourful city with lots of places where you can relax. There are a lot of picturesque streets, churches and museums, not to mention the lovely City Park.

What do you miss the most about your home town?
Friends, family and the sunshine!

What is the main football stadium like there?
Debrecen play at the Olah Gabor Stadion. There is talk of it being redeveloped into a much more modern ground.

What other sports are popular there?
Football is the No.1 sport in Hungary, but we are also good at kayaking, fencing and canoeing. Swimming has also produced a lot of success, and Hungary has won Olympic golds in watersports.

Describe something you can buy in your home town which you can't get in Edinburgh?
Hungarian goulash! The really traditional dish is a soup made with beef, potato, dumplings and vegetables.

Michael Stewart

FAMILY FORTUNES

Dylan McGowan came over to Edinburgh from Australia for a holiday – and ended up signing for Hearts.

The young Jambo had made the trip to visit his elder brother Ryan, who had been recruited by the Edinburgh club from hometown club Para Hills in Adelaide. Little did he realise, however, that his jaunt to the Capital would lead to such a sporting adventure.

"Hearts knew about me before I came over, and when I did visit my brother, the club decided I might as well have a trial when I was here," said Dylan.

"It all worked out well. I have really enjoyed it since I came, and it was certainly easier to settle in having the big brother here. He's a lot older so I try to take in what he has to say."

The brothers played together for the first time in a Reserve League clash last season when Hearts defeated Celtic 3-2 at Forthbank Stadium in April. That experience will linger long in their minds, and they plan to have many more such highlights with Hearts in the future.

"We actually played together for the first time at Hearts in a reserve game against Celtic last season, which was a great experience," added Dylan.

"The ambition is to break into the first team, but for now I just want to play regularly in the U19s and break into the Reserves."

The Aussie duo both prefer to play at centre-half and Ryan admitted their rivalry has been beneficial to their careers. "Dylan arrived over two years ago when he came over to see me on a holiday," said Ryan.

"I told Darren Murray about him, and he said if he had some spare time just to get him to the academy. He played a few games and ended up signing.

"It's good rivalry as we try to push each other to be better, and last season we played a few reserve games together, which was good.

"We have a good understanding as we have watched each other play since we were younger, so it's been good to finally come to a big club and play in games like this as it's what we have dreamed of since we were five or six years old.

"...it's what we have dreamed of since we were five or six years old."

"I think my best position is centre-back, but I do enjoy centre midfield as well. I'll play anywhere really. I don't mind as long as I am on the pitch."

Ryan, 20, played a leading role as the Reserves clinched second place in the SPL Reserve League, while his younger brother missed just one game as the U19s secured runners-up spot in the Clydesdale Bank U19 League.

"To come second in the Reserve League is a big achievement," added Ryan.

"It's not the same team every week, and one game you might be up against an experienced side and the next it might be more from the U19s.

"It was good last season that the 19s finished second as well, and that can only be good for the future."

"It's good rivalry as we try to push each other to be better..."

GUESS WHO?

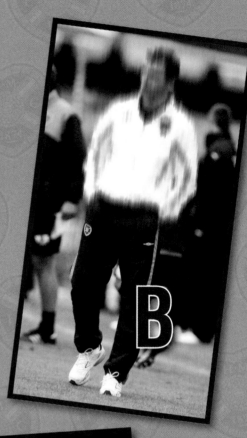

Answers on page 61.

J is for Jim Jefferies, Scottish Cup-winning manager of 1998.

A is for Alfie Conn, Gorgie legend.

M is for magnificent 08-09 season.

B is for best of the rest.

O is for one true love.

S is for seven Scottish Cup triumphs.

TUNNEL VISION

Rising star Craig Thomson is dreaming of the day he runs out in front of a packed Tynecastle Stadium.

Voted last season's U19 Player of the Year, the full-back is highly rated by the club's coaching staff and signed a new three-year contract in May which will see him remain in Gorgie until the summer of 2012.

The youngster is one of the many quality players to be produced by the academy, and, while delighted with his progress so far, the 18-year-old remains focused on achieving his ultimate target of first team football in the near future.

"I've still got another year left at U19s level so I'm just looking to keep progressing at the club," he said.

"It would be unbelievable to one day run out of the tunnel to play for the team at Tynecastle in a stadium full of Hearts fans."

Signed as an 11-year-old from a local boys club, the defender learned a lot from Robbie Neilson while he revealed that Jason Thomson has also had a significant influence on him.

A frequent goal-scorer for both the 19s and Reserves last season despite his full-back role, Thomson believes Hearts is the perfect club for young players to thrive.

"I was on the free-kicks and penalties last season which helped, but it's always good to see your name on the score sheet, and that helps your confidence," he said.

"Robbie Neilson was a massive influence on me, especially with him being captain.

"I have to mention Jason Thomson as well. He has come through the ranks and knows what it's like and has always been great with advice.

"It would be unbelievable to one day run out of the tunnel to play for the team at Tynecastle in a stadium full of Hearts fans."

"The quality coming through the academy seems to be getting better and better. It's a great club for young players and we know we'll get a chance if we keep performing well.

"I want to keep getting better and better and think I can do that here."

Team-mates Calum Elliot and Gary Glen have certainly blossomed during their time at Tynecastle after savouring their big breakthrough, with Craig adding: "Calum did really well after coming back from his loan at Livingston last season, and guys like Gary Glen are just waiting for opportunities, so hopefully all the younger players are driven on to better things after seeing how well they have done.

"I know, though, that I will have to keep doing well for the U19s and then the reserves to get that opportunity."

SPOT the BALL

Can you spot the ball?

Answers on page 61.

WORD SEARCH

```
B M T P I T C H O H L T
Y P A M G O R G I E C P
S Y E T D S M A R I A L
T I U Z C N T O R H D A
E F R L B H T A J M R Y
A G O W T S E R D B C E
M H P S R I R S S Z R
E D E E N A C T T Y U S
R J P H J A D K F M F M
P U T U N N E L E O E Y
S O D O G F M C R T Y E
Y C Y G Z L D Q T C S S
```

GORGIE   SUPERSTORE   TICKETS   MATCHES   TUNNEL

PITCH   PLAYERS   STADIUM   TEAM   EUROPE

Answers on page 61.

FOREIGN STARS

RICARDO FULLER

The Jamaican helped bring some Caribbean sunshine to Tynecastle and scored some memorable goals in maroon while on loan before moving to England.

BORN: Kingston, Jamaica, October 31, 1979.
DEBUT: October 21, 2001 (h) Hibs (SPL 1-2)
CAREER:
» 2001: Tivoli Gardens.
» 2001-02: Crystal Palace.
» 2001-02: Hearts (loan).
» 2002: Preston North End.
» 2004: Portsmouth.
» 2005: Southampton.
» 2006: Ipswich (loan).
» 2006: Stoke City.

MICHAL POSPISIL

The Czech striker will be remembered as the player who kept his nerve to slot home the winning penalty in the 2006 Scottish Cup Final shoot-out against Gretna.

BORN: Prague, March 5, 1979.
DEBUT: August 14, 2006 (a), Dundee United (SPL 3-0).
CAREER:
» 1995: Sparta Prague.
» 2000: Viktoria Zizkov.
» 2002: Sparta Prague.
» 2003: Slovan Liberec.
» 2005: Hearts.
» 2008: K. Sint-Truidense V.V.
» 2009: Viktoria Zizkov.

THOMAS FLOGEL

The Austrian became one of the most popular foreign players to pull on the famous Maroon jersey, his crowning moment coming with the Scottish Cup victory over Rangers in 1998.

BORN: Vienna, June 7, 1971.
DEBUT: August 4, 1997 (a), Rangers (PL 1-3)
CAREER:
» 1990: Austria Vienna.
» 1997: Hearts.
» 2002: Austria Vienna.
» 2004: Pasching.
» 2005: Admira Wacker.
» 2006: Vienna FC; retired after a shoulder injury.

KEVIN McKENNA

The Canadian international proved his versatility during his four-year spell at Tynecastle, playing in a number of positions for the Maroons.

BORN: Calgary, January 21, 1980.
DEBUT: March 18, 2001 (a) Dundee (SPL 0-0).
CAREER:
» 1998: Energie Cottbus.
» 2001: Hearts.
» 2005: Energie Cottbus.
» 2007: FC Koln.

HUSREF MUSEMIC

Hearts' first Yugoslavian signing, 'Moose' is best remembered by supporters for heading the winner against Hibs in his one and only derby appearance.

BORN: Janja, Yugoslavia, July 4, 1961.
DEBUT: Celtic (h), August 12, 1989 (PL 1-3).
CAREER:
» Red Star Belgrade.
» 1989: Hearts.
» 1990: Sarajevo.

ANTTI NIEMI

The Finn was hugely popular with the fans during his time in Gorgie, his form between the posts quickly establishing him as a Tynecastle favourite.

BORN: Oulu, May 31, 1972.
DEBUT: December 19, 1999 (h), Hibs (SPL 0-3).
CAREER:
» 1996: FC Copenhagen.
» 1997: Rangers.
» 1999: Charlton.
» 1999: Hearts.
» 2002: Southampton.
» 2006: Fulham: January 10; retired due to injury in September 2008.

PASQUALE BRUNO

His aggressive style earned him many admirers in Gorgie, and he was a key performer for the Edinburgh club during Jim Jefferies' time in charge.

BORN: Lecce, Italy, June 1962.
DEBUT: November 4, 1995 (h), Partick Thistle (PL 3-0).
CAREER:
» 1979: Lecce.
» 1983: Como.
» 1987: Juventus.
» 1990: Torino.
» 1993: Fiorentina.
» 1995: Lecce.
» 1994: Hearts.
» 1997: Wigan.

HEARTS JUNIORS

HEARTS JUNIORS

HEARTS JUNIOR MEMBERSHIP IS FREE!

FOLLOW YOUR HEARTS...

QUIZ ANSWERS

Word Search from page 21

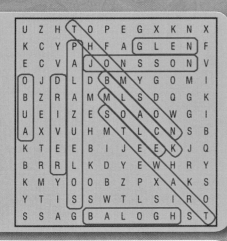

Maze to Tynecastle from page 26

Annual Quiz from page 30

1. Motherwell
2. Michael Stewart
3. It was Hearts' 5th straight league win of the season
4. 16
5. Arvydas Novikovas
6. Wolverhampton Wanderers
7. 4
8. Hamilton
9. Pittodrie
10. 3

Spot the Difference from page 35

Word Search from page 42

GUESS WHO? from page 52

A. Ian Black
B. Csaba Lazlo
C. Michael Stewart
D. Ruben Palazuelos

Word Search from page 57

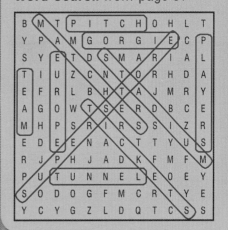

Spot the Ball from page 56